CHECK
REGISTER

NAME: ______________________________

PHONE: ______________________________

STARTING BALANCE ____________

Date	Code/#	Description	Payment Debit (-)		Payment Credit (+)		Balance	

STARTING BALANCE ____________

Date	Code/#	Description	Payment Debit (-)		Payment Credit (+)		Balance	

STARTING BALANCE ___________

Date	Code/#	Description	Payment Debit (-)		Payment Credit (+)		Balance	

STARTING BALANCE ____________

Date	Code/#	Description	Payment Debit (-)		Payment Credit (+)		Balance	

STARTING BALANCE ____________

Date	Code/#	Description	Payment Debit (-)		Payment Credit (+)		Balance	

STARTING BALANCE ____________

Date	Code/#	Description	Payment Debit (-)		Payment Credit (+)		Balance	

STARTING BALANCE ____________

Date	Code/#	Description	Payment Debit (-)		Payment Credit (+)		Balance	

STARTING BALANCE ____________

Date	Code/#	Description	Payment Debit (-)		Payment Credit (+)		Balance	

STARTING BALANCE ____________

Date	Code/#	Description	Payment Debit (-)		Payment Credit (+)		Balance	

STARTING BALANCE ____________

Date	Code/#	Description	Payment Debit (-)		Payment Credit (+)		Balance	

STARTING BALANCE ____________

Date	Code/#	Description	Payment Debit (-)		Payment Credit (+)		Balance	

STARTING BALANCE ___________

Date	Code/#	Description	Payment Debit (-)		Payment Credit (+)		Balance	

STARTING BALANCE ____________

Date	Code/#	Description	Payment Debit (-)		Payment Credit (+)		Balance	

STARTING BALANCE ____________

Date	Code/#	Description	Payment Debit (-)		Payment Credit (+)		Balance	

STARTING BALANCE ____________

Date	Code/#	Description	Payment Debit (-)		Payment Credit (+)		Balance	

STARTING BALANCE ____________

Date	Code/#	Description	Payment Debit (-)		Payment Credit (+)		Balance	

STARTING BALANCE ____________

Date	Code/#	Description	Payment Debit (-)		Payment Credit (+)		Balance	

STARTING BALANCE ____________

Date	Code/#	Description	Payment Debit (-)		Payment Credit (+)		Balance	

STARTING BALANCE ____________

Date	Code/#	Description	Payment Debit (-)		Payment Credit (+)		Balance	

STARTING BALANCE ____________

Date	Code/#	Description	Payment Debit (-)		Payment Credit (+)		Balance	

STARTING BALANCE ____________

Date	Code/#	Description	Payment Debit (-)		Payment Credit (+)		Balance	

STARTING BALANCE ____________

Date	Code/#	Description	Payment Debit (-)		Payment Credit (+)		Balance	

STARTING BALANCE ____________

Date	Code/#	Description	Payment Debit (-)	Payment Credit (+)	Balance

STARTING BALANCE ____________

Date	Code/#	Description	Payment Debit (-)		Payment Credit (+)		Balance	

STARTING BALANCE ____________

Date	Code/#	Description	Payment Debit (-)		Payment Credit (+)		Balance	

STARTING BALANCE ____________

Date	Code/#	Description	Payment Debit (-)		Payment Credit (+)		Balance	

STARTING BALANCE ____________

Date	Code/#	Description	Payment Debit (-)		Payment Credit (+)		Balance	

STARTING BALANCE ____________

Date	Code/#	Description	Payment Debit (-)		Payment Credit (+)		Balance	

STARTING BALANCE ____________

Date	Code/#	Description	Payment Debit (-)		Payment Credit (+)		Balance	

STARTING BALANCE ____________

Date	Code/#	Description	Payment Debit (-)		Payment Credit (+)		Balance	

STARTING BALANCE ____________

Date	Code/#	Description	Payment Debit (-)		Payment Credit (+)		Balance	

STARTING BALANCE ____________

Date	Code/#	Description	Payment Debit (-)		Payment Credit (+)		Balance	

STARTING BALANCE ____________

Date	Code/#	Description	Payment Debit (-)		Payment Credit (+)		Balance	

STARTING BALANCE ____________

Date	Code/#	Description	Payment Debit (-)		Payment Credit (+)		Balance	

STARTING BALANCE ____________

Date	Code/#	Description	Payment Debit (-)	Payment Credit (+)	Balance

STARTING BALANCE ____________

Date	Code/#	Description	Payment Debit (-)		Payment Credit (+)		Balance	

STARTING BALANCE ____________

Date	Code/#	Description	Payment Debit (-)		Payment Credit (+)		Balance	

STARTING BALANCE ____________

Date	Code/#	Description	Payment Debit (-)		Payment Credit (+)		Balance	

STARTING BALANCE ____________

Date	Code/#	Description	Payment Debit (-)		Payment Credit (+)		Balance	

STARTING BALANCE ____________

Date	Code/#	Description	Payment Debit (-)		Payment Credit (+)		Balance	

STARTING BALANCE ____________

Date	Code/#	Description	Payment Debit (-)		Payment Credit (+)		Balance	

STARTING BALANCE ____________

Date	Code/#	Description	Payment Debit (-)		Payment Credit (+)		Balance	

STARTING BALANCE ____________

Date	Code/#	Description	Payment Debit (-)		Payment Credit (+)		Balance	

STARTING BALANCE ____________

Date	Code/#	Description	Payment Debit (-)		Payment Credit (+)		Balance	

STARTING BALANCE ____________

Date	Code/#	Description	Payment Debit (-)		Payment Credit (+)		Balance	

STARTING BALANCE ____________

Date	Code/#	Description	Payment Debit (-)		Payment Credit (+)		Balance	

STARTING BALANCE ____________

Date	Code/#	Description	Payment Debit (-)		Payment Credit (+)		Balance	

STARTING BALANCE ____________

Date	Code/#	Description	Payment Debit (-)		Payment Credit (+)		Balance	

STARTING BALANCE ____________

Date	Code/#	Description	Payment Debit (-)		Payment Credit (+)		Balance	

STARTING BALANCE ____________

Date	Code/#	Description	Payment Debit (-)		Payment Credit (+)		Balance	

STARTING BALANCE ____________

Date	Code/#	Description	Payment Debit (-)		Payment Credit (+)		Balance	

STARTING BALANCE ____________

Date	Code/#	Description	Payment Debit (-)		Payment Credit (+)		Balance	

STARTING BALANCE ___________

Date	Code/#	Description	Payment Debit (-)		Payment Credit (+)		Balance	

STARTING BALANCE ___________

Date	Code/#	Description	Payment Debit (-)		Payment Credit (+)		Balance	

STARTING BALANCE ____________

Date	Code/#	Description	Payment Debit (-)		Payment Credit (+)		Balance	

STARTING BALANCE ____________

Date	Code/#	Description	Payment Debit (-)		Payment Credit (+)		Balance	

STARTING BALANCE ____________

Date	Code/#	Description	Payment Debit (-)		Payment Credit (+)		Balance	

STARTING BALANCE ____________

Date	Code/#	Description	Payment Debit (-)		Payment Credit (+)		Balance	

STARTING BALANCE ____________

Date	Code/#	Description	Payment Debit (-)		Payment Credit (+)		Balance	

STARTING BALANCE ____________

Date	Code/#	Description	Payment Debit (-)		Payment Credit (+)		Balance	

STARTING BALANCE ____________

Date	Code/#	Description	Payment Debit (-)		Payment Credit (+)		Balance	

STARTING BALANCE ____________

Date	Code/#	Description	Payment Debit (-)		Payment Credit (+)		Balance	

STARTING BALANCE ____________

Date	Code/#	Description	Payment Debit (-)	Payment Credit (+)	Balance

STARTING BALANCE ____________

Date	Code/#	Description	Payment Debit (-)		Payment Credit (+)		Balance	

STARTING BALANCE ____________

Date	Code/#	Description	Payment Debit (-)		Payment Credit (+)		Balance	

STARTING BALANCE ____________

Date	Code/#	Description	Payment Debit (-)		Payment Credit (+)		Balance	

STARTING BALANCE ____________

Date	Code/#	Description	Payment Debit (-)		Payment Credit (+)		Balance	

STARTING BALANCE ____________

Date	Code/#	Description	Payment Debit (-)		Payment Credit (+)		Balance	

STARTING BALANCE ___________

Date	Code/#	Description	Payment Debit (-)		Payment Credit (+)		Balance	

STARTING BALANCE ____________

Date	Code/#	Description	Payment Debit (-)		Payment Credit (+)		Balance	

STARTING BALANCE ____________

Date	Code/#	Description	Payment Debit (-)		Payment Credit (+)		Balance	

STARTING BALANCE ____________

Date	Code/#	Description	Payment Debit (-)		Payment Credit (+)		Balance	

STARTING BALANCE ____________

Date	Code/#	Description	Payment Debit (-)		Payment Credit (+)		Balance	

STARTING BALANCE ____________

Date	Code/#	Description	Payment Debit (-)		Payment Credit (+)		Balance	

STARTING BALANCE ____________

Date	Code/#	Description	Payment Debit (-)		Payment Credit (+)		Balance	

STARTING BALANCE ____________

Date	Code/#	Description	Payment Debit (-)		Payment Credit (+)		Balance	

STARTING BALANCE ____________

Date	Code/#	Description	Payment Debit (-)		Payment Credit (+)		Balance	

STARTING BALANCE ____________

Date	Code/#	Description	Payment Debit (-)		Payment Credit (+)		Balance	

STARTING BALANCE ____________

Date	Code/#	Description	Payment Debit (-)		Payment Credit (+)		Balance	

STARTING BALANCE ____________

Date	Code/#	Description	Payment Debit (-)	Payment Credit (+)	Balance

STARTING BALANCE ____________

Date	Code/#	Description	Payment Debit (-)		Payment Credit (+)		Balance	

STARTING BALANCE ____________

Date	Code/#	Description	Payment Debit (-)		Payment Credit (+)		Balance	

STARTING BALANCE ____________

Date	Code/#	Description	Payment Debit (-)		Payment Credit (+)		Balance	

STARTING BALANCE ____________

Date	Code/#	Description	Payment Debit (-)		Payment Credit (+)		Balance	

STARTING BALANCE ____________

Date	Code/#	Description	Payment Debit (-)		Payment Credit (+)		Balance	

STARTING BALANCE ___________

Date	Code/#	Description	Payment Debit (-)		Payment Credit (+)		Balance	

STARTING BALANCE ____________

Date	Code/#	Description	Payment Debit (-)		Payment Credit (+)		Balance	

STARTING BALANCE ____________

Date	Code/#	Description	Payment Debit (-)		Payment Credit (+)		Balance	

STARTING BALANCE ____________

Date	Code/#	Description	Payment Debit (-)		Payment Credit (+)		Balance	

STARTING BALANCE ____________

Date	Code/#	Description	Payment Debit (-)		Payment Credit (+)		Balance	

STARTING BALANCE ____________

Date	Code/#	Description	Payment Debit (-)		Payment Credit (+)		Balance	

STARTING BALANCE ____________

Date	Code/#	Description	Payment Debit (-)		Payment Credit (+)		Balance	

STARTING BALANCE ____________

Date	Code/#	Description	Payment Debit (-)		Payment Credit (+)		Balance	

STARTING BALANCE ____________

Date	Code/#	Description	Payment Debit (-)		Payment Credit (+)		Balance	

STARTING BALANCE ____________

Date	Code/#	Description	Payment Debit (-)		Payment Credit (+)		Balance	

STARTING BALANCE ____________

Date	Code/#	Description	Payment Debit (-)		Payment Credit (+)		Balance	

STARTING BALANCE ____________

Date	Code/#	Description	Payment Debit (-)		Payment Credit (+)		Balance	

STARTING BALANCE ____________

Date	Code/#	Description	Payment Debit (-)		Payment Credit (+)		Balance	

STARTING BALANCE ____________

Date	Code/#	Description	Payment Debit (-)		Payment Credit (+)		Balance	

STARTING BALANCE ____________

Date	Code/#	Description	Payment Debit (-)		Payment Credit (+)		Balance	

STARTING BALANCE ____________

Date	Code/#	Description	Payment Debit (-)		Payment Credit (+)		Balance	

STARTING BALANCE ____________

Date	Code/#	Description	Payment Debit (-)		Payment Credit (+)		Balance	

STARTING BALANCE ____________

Date	Code/#	Description	Payment Debit (-)		Payment Credit (+)		Balance	

STARTING BALANCE ______________

Date	Code/#	Description	Payment Debit (-)		Payment Credit (+)		Balance	

STARTING BALANCE ___________

Date	Code/#	Description	Payment Debit (-)		Payment Credit (+)		Balance	

STARTING BALANCE ____________

Date	Code/#	Description	Payment Debit (-)		Payment Credit (+)		Balance	

STARTING BALANCE ____________

Date	Code/#	Description	Payment Debit (-)		Payment Credit (+)		Balance	

STARTING BALANCE ____________

Date	Code/#	Description	Payment Debit (-)		Payment Credit (+)		Balance	

STARTING BALANCE ____________

Date	Code/#	Description	Payment Debit (-)		Payment Credit (+)		Balance	

STARTING BALANCE ____________

Date	Code/#	Description	Payment Debit (-)		Payment Credit (+)		Balance	

STARTING BALANCE ____________

Date	Code/#	Description	Payment Debit (-)		Payment Credit (+)		Balance	

STARTING BALANCE ____________

Date	Code/#	Description	Payment Debit (-)		Payment Credit (+)		Balance	

STARTING BALANCE ____________

Date	Code/#	Description	Payment Debit (-)		Payment Credit (+)		Balance	

STARTING BALANCE ____________

Date	Code/#	Description	Payment Debit (-)		Payment Credit (+)		Balance	

STARTING BALANCE ____________

Date	Code/#	Description	Payment Debit (-)		Payment Credit (+)		Balance	

STARTING BALANCE ____________

Date	Code/#	Description	Payment Debit (-)		Payment Credit (+)		Balance	

STARTING BALANCE ____________

Date	Code/#	Description	Payment Debit (-)		Payment Credit (+)		Balance	

STARTING BALANCE ____________

Date	Code/#	Description	Payment Debit (-)		Payment Credit (+)		Balance	

STARTING BALANCE ____________

Date	Code/#	Description	Payment Debit (-)		Payment Credit (+)		Balance	

CPSIA information can be obtained
at www.ICGtesting.com
Printed in the USA
LVHW050308050321
680568LV00018B/594

9 780800 113377